DATE DUE

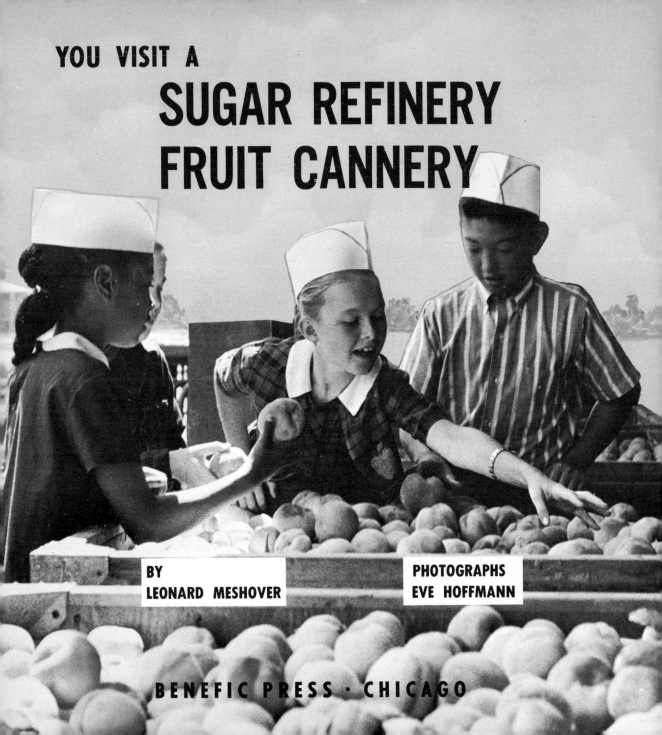

YOU VISIT A
SUGAR REFINERY
FRUIT CANNERY

BY
LEONARD MESHOVER

PHOTOGRAPHS
EVE HOFFMANN

BENEFIC PRESS · CHICAGO

URBAN LIVING SERIES

Acknowledgment for assistance in obtaining
photographs is made to the following:

C and H Sugar Company

Dole Company

CONTENTS

WHAT WILL WE SEE AT THE SUGAR REFINERY?

We will see how sugar is refined today. The sugar that we eat is refined.

What is raw sugar? Where does the refinery get the raw sugar?

There are big bins at the refinery. Do you know what they are used for?

Sugar comes in many kinds of packages. Maybe we will see some of them.

SUGAR COMES TO THE REFINERY

Hello, children.
This is the sugar
refinery.
Come right in.

First we will see where the ships come in. There you will see the raw sugar as it comes to us. Ships bring raw sugar here from Hawaii.

This ship came in from Hawaii just this morning.
Come. We will go on it.

You can see how the ship has been made just for carrying sugar.

The raw sugar will go from the ship into large bins outside the refinery.

Now look at the bins. Each one is six stories high. The raw sugar is stored in them until it goes into the refinery.

9

Here we are at the very top of the bins. We can look down on the raw sugar inside. The sugar you see here has been taken from the ship we were just on.

This is how the raw
sugar goes from the
bins into the refinery. It
is carried along on this
moving belt.

This sugar doesn't
look much like the
sugar we eat at home.

It soon will, children.

REFINING THE RAW SUGAR

The raw sugar has been melted into a syrup so that the non-sugars can be taken out. Then the syrup is heated until sugar crystals form again.

Look in here. You can see sugar crystals forming at the bottom of the syrup.

12

In this machine the syrup is spun away from the sugar crystals.

Look in here. This machine dries the sugar crystals. When the crystals are dry, the sugar is refined. It is now ready to eat.

THE SUGAR IS PACKAGED

The refined sugar must be put into packages. Here brown sugar is going into the boxes. Maybe your mother will buy one of them at the store.

Look at these little packages of sugar!
They are used in restaurants, children.

We use machines to move the big packages of sugar.
Smaller packages are inside these large ones.

The packaged sugar is stored until it is sent out.
It will go to stores in many parts of our country.

17

I can move these heavy
packages of sugar, too.
Look out. Here I come!

18

SUGAR IN THE KITCHEN

This is our test kitchen, children. Here we work out new and better ways to use sugar.

Would you like to make some cookies?

I'll put in the sugar.

Oh, the cookies look good.
They taste good, too.

Would you like to try one of our cookies? We just made them.

Thank you. I know they will taste good.

FOR A BETTER REFINERY

This new machine will
soon be ready to use.
It will help us to
package the sugar faster.

Would you like to help
us put in our new
machine? First you must
put this on your head.
It will help keep you safe
when you work.

My work is part of sugar refining, too. I look for new and better ways to refine sugar.

WHAT DID WE SEE AT THE SUGAR REFINERY?

We saw the raw sugar as it comes from Hawaii. We saw how the raw sugar is melted so that the non-sugars can be taken out. After the sugar crystals were dried, we saw the refined sugar put into packages.

We went to the test kitchen and made some cookies. We saw a man working to find new and better ways to refine sugar.

And before we went home, we got some sugar to take with us.

WHAT WILL WE SEE AT THE FRUIT CANNERY?

We will visit a fruit cannery today. Do you know what kind of fruit is canned at the cannery?

It is fruit cocktail. We will see how fruit cocktail is canned.

What fruits are used in fruit cocktail?

How is the fruit cocktail put into the cans?

Will there be fruit juice at the cannery?

We will soon see.

Come on. Let's go!

FRUIT FOR THE CANNERY

Oh, look. Here is a machine with fruit juice from the cannery. Let's have some before we start our visit.

First we will see the fruit as it comes to the cannery. Grapes, peaches, pears, cherries, and pineapple are the fruits used in fruit cocktail.

Here are some grapes that have just come in. Soon they will go into the cannery.

Here are some peaches that just came in.
Don't they look good?

IN THE CANNERY

Now the peaches are coming into the cannery. Moving belts bring them in. The peaches will be washed and peeled right away.

30

Any peaches that have not been all peeled are taken out. Peaches too ripe for canning are also taken out.

Here come the grapes.

Moving belts bring them into the cannery. Only the best grapes will be canned. The others are taken out.

The grapes in these pans are ready
to be put with the other fruits
in the fruit cocktail.

Here are the cherries that will go into the fruit cocktail. Only the best ones will be canned.

34

Don't these look good?
Wouldn't you like to eat some now?

See this machine. It peels the pears.

Hello, children. My work is to cut away any part of the pear that is too ripe for canning.

Does this pineapple go into the fruit cocktail, too?

Yes, it does. It comes to us in cans from Hawaii.

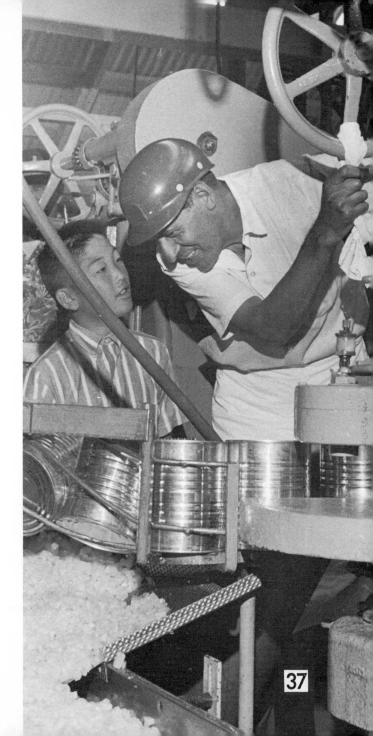

37

CANNED FRUIT

Look at all the cans!

Yes, this is where we store the cans. Soon they will be filled with fruit cocktail.

38

Moving belts take the cans
to the fruit.
Down come the cans.

These cans have been
filled. Soon they will be
covered and sealed.

The sealed cans are heated
in this big machine. The
heating keeps the fruit pure
inside the cans.

41

Now the labels are being put on the cans.
See how fast they go!

The cans of fruit cocktail are ready to be
packed now.

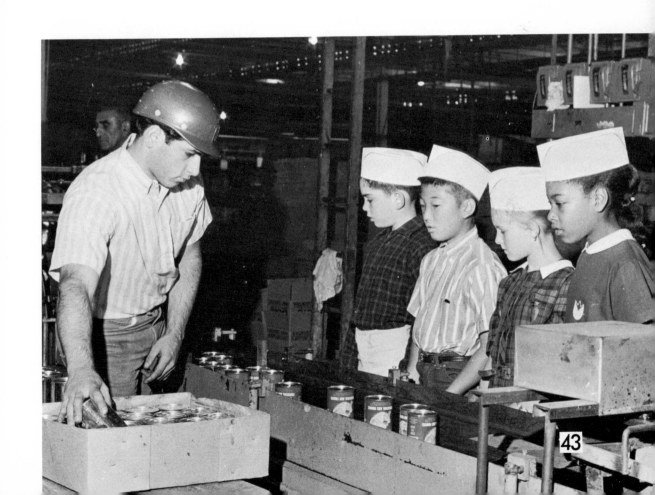

Let's help put away the packed boxes for storing.
Oh, oh! These are heavy.

FRUIT COCKTAIL TO EAT

Do you work with fruit cocktail, too?

Yes, I do. My work is to find ways to make fruit cocktail even better than it is.

This is our test kitchen, children. Would you like
to taste this pie? It has a fruit cocktail topping.

WHAT DID WE SEE AT THE FRUIT CANNERY?

We saw the fruit as it comes to the cannery. The pineapple and cherries came in cans. The other fruit was fresh.

We saw the fruit as it was peeled and cleaned. After that, it was put into cans. We helped pack some cans of fruit cocktail.

And we will have fruit cocktail to eat at home!

47

Vocabulary

The total number of different words used in this book is 197. Of these, twenty-five words, listed below in roman type, are second-grade level. Twenty-four words, shown below in italics, are above second-grade level. The words are listed in alphabetical order,and the number after the word indicates the page on which it first appears.

also 31

belt 11
bins 4
bottom 12

cannery 26
cherries 28
cocktail 26
cookies 19
crystals 12

doesn't 11
dries 13

even 45

form 12

grapes 28

heated 12
heavy 18

juice 26

kitchen 19

labels 42
large 9

machine 13
maybe 4
melted 12

non-sugars 12

outside 9

packages 4
packed 43
pans 33
parts 16
peaches 28
pears 28
peeled 30

pie 46
pineapple 28
pure 40

raw 4
refined 4
refinery 4
restaurants 15
ripe 31

safe 23
sealed 40
sent 16
ships 6
spun 13
sugar 4

taken 10
taste 21
test 19

wouldn't 35

JFMAMJJASOND–71706968676 6